D1208161

Careers For
Animal
Lovers

Interviews by Russell Shorto

Photographs by Edward Keating and Carrie Boretz

92 06500

CHOICES
The Millbrook Press
Brookfield, Connecticut

Produced in association with Agincourt Press.

Choices Editor: Megan Liberman

Photographs by Edward Keating, except: Joy Gonzalez
(Carrie Boretz), Craig Chittenden (Carrie Boretz),
Okeefenokee Joe (Myra Johns), Laurel Wright (Jim Berry),
Tufail Mohammed (Carrie Boretz), Dan Wharton (Carrie Boretz),
Felicitas Camacho (Steve Kagan).

Library of Congress Cataloging-in-Publication Data

Shorto, Russell.
Careers for animal lovers/interviews by Russell Shorto,
photographs by Edward Keating and Carrie Boretz.

p.   cm. – (Choices)
Includes bibliographical references and index.

Summary: Includes interviews with people who hold such varied
careers as animal illustrator, pet store owner, dairy farmer, and
zoo biologist, telling what they do, how they got started, and
the necessary preparation for each job.

ISBN 1-56294-160-7

1. Animal welfare – Vocational guidance – United States – Juvenile
literature.   2. Animal culture – Vocational guidance – United
States – Juvenile literature.   3. Animal specialists – Vocational
guidance – United States – Juvenile literature.   4. Animal
rights – Vocational guidance – United States – Juvenile literature.
[1. Zoology – Vocational guidance.   2. Vocational guidance.
3. Occupations.]
I. Keating, Edward, ill.   II. Boretz, Carrie, ill.
III. Title.   IV. Series: Choices (Brookfield, Conn.)
HV4764.S53   1992   91-27657
636'.0023'73 – dc20

Photographs copyright in the names of the photographers.

Copyright © 1992 by The Millbrook Press
All rights reserved
Printed in the United States of America
6 5 4 3 2 1

CENTRAL ARKANSAS LIBRARY SYSTEM
ADOLPHINE FLETCHER TERRY BRANCH
LITTLE ROCK, ARKANSAS

Contents

Introduction

In this book, fourteen men and women who work in animal-related fields talk about their careers — what their work involves, how they got started, and what they like (and dislike) about it. They tell you things you should know before beginning an animal-related career and show you how a love of animals can lead to many different types of jobs.

Some of the people profiled in this book care for animals directly, such as the veterinarian, animal shelter foreman, and zoo keeper. Others — such as the wildlife conservationist, zoo biologist, and game warden — work to protect the rights of animals worldwide. Still others educate the public about animals, the snake handler and marine mammal trainer among them.

The fourteen careers described here are just the beginning, so don't limit your sights. At the end of this book, you'll find short descriptions of a dozen more careers you may want to explore, as well as suggestions on how to get more information. There are many business opportunities that involve working with animals. If you enjoy this kind of work, you'll find a wide range of career choices open to you.

Joan E. Storey, M.B.A., M.S.W.
Series Career Consultant

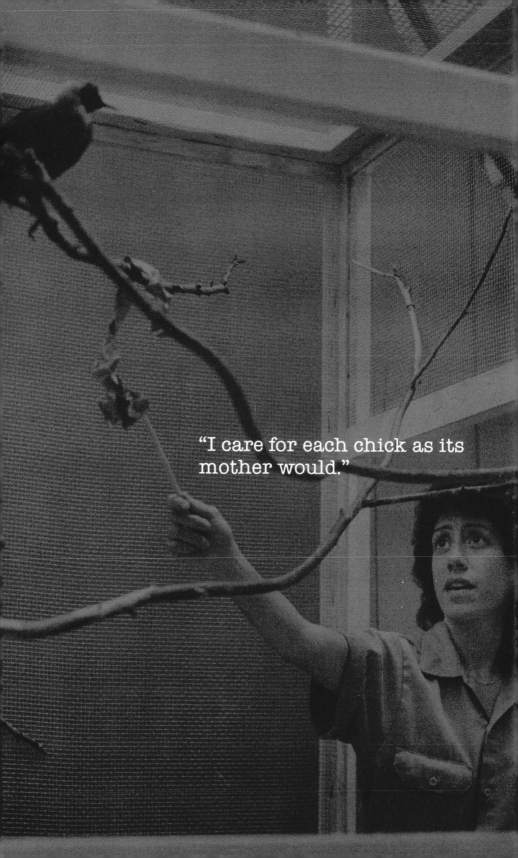

"I care for each chick as its mother would."

JOY GONZALEZ
ZOO KEEPER
New York, New York

WHAT I DO:

As the senior bird keeper at a city zoo, I hand-rear endangered species of birds. The zoo is divided into different departments, such as the mammal, reptile, and bird departments. Within the bird department, we have about twenty keepers working at different locations. I'm the primary keeper in the brooder room, where chicks are reared.

When it comes to breeding animals in captivity, we don't take any chances on first-time parents rearing their young. They may toss a chick out of the nest. So, we remove each egg and incubate it. Then, when the chick hatches, I feed and care for it as its mother would. I work with several species of birds, including cranes, pheasants, and the Mauritius pink

Joy lures one of the birds from its cage for a feeding.

pigeon. Probably our most spectacular success has been with the bird of paradise, a rare bird native to New Guinea. It's endangered because people kill it for its beautiful plumes.

I start work at 8:00 A.M. I'll begin by weighing the chicks to make sure they're doing well. Then I feed them. The altricial chicks – those born without feathers – get fed about every two hours, so I feed them throughout the day. Precocial chicks, however – those born with downy feathers, such as pheasants and ducks – eat on their own by the second day. They're more alert and require less attention.

The rest of my day is spent cleaning, feeding, and monitoring the health of the birds. The vets come by every day or two to check on the birds themselves, and when we have chicks with problems, I'm also responsible

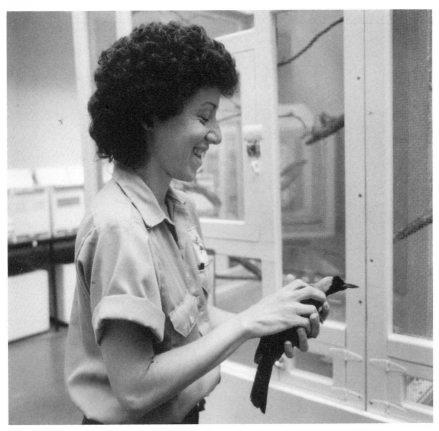

Joy holds one of the birds in the brooder room.

for medicating them. My work day ends at 5:00 P.M.

HOW I GOT STARTED:
I had lots and lots of pets as a child — dogs, birds, anything really — and I studied biology in college because I've always wanted to work with animals. After college, I took a job at the zoo in visitor services, just to get in. From there, I got a position in the children's zoo for a summer, and then I volunteered for the bird department. When an opening for a keeper came up, I was hired. Now I'm working on my master's degree in biopsychology, which is the study of animal behavior.

HOW I FEEL ABOUT IT:
I've had the opportunity to do a lot of wonderful things. It's very rewarding to rear a chick from birth and finally see it eating on its own. There are frustrations, however, such as when a chick get sick. This can be emotionally stressful. If you've raised a chick for six months and

then it dies, that's really hard to take.

Trying to get a bird to eat on its own also requires a lot of patience. There's no way for a human to show a bird how to eat. It's not like in nature, where a mother can teach by example. You have to do it differently. We feed them with forceps. Then, as they get older, we reduce the amount of hand-feeds and coax them to the food pan.

WHAT YOU SHOULD KNOW: Volunteering to work for a zoo is a very good way to break in. Most zoos are happy to take volunteers. You can observe the keepers and learn what kind of animals you like to work with. Also, if a job becomes available, you'll have an advantage because you're already there, and people will know you and how you work.

Zoos require an advanced degree for upper-level positions. If you're interested in mammals, you might take courses in mammology. If you're interested in birds, take ornithology. But don't limit yourself. The competition for jobs in zoos is stiff, so it's important to be open to working in any department. If I had only wanted to work with mammals, I might not have gotten a job.

The pay scale varies with the zoo because small zoos can't pay as much as large zoos. A starting salary for a keeper at a big zoo might be in the $24,000-a-year range. But you can quickly move up from starting keeper to regular keeper to senior keeper. A senior keeper starts at about $27,000 a year.

Joy hand-feeds one of the many birds in her care.

"My cows are like my best friends."

CRAIG CHITTENDEN

DAIRY FARMER

Stephentown, New York

WHAT I DO:

I own and operate a dairy farm – which, simply put, means that I milk cows for a living. I do just about everything myself, though my wife and two children lend a hand. I also hire some part-time people to help out here and there.

The farm is nine years old, which is pretty new for a dairy farm. We have about 110 Jersey cows and 80 heifers, or young cows, for replacement stock. The whole farm is about 280 acres, of which 110 are tillable. Land is called tillable if you can grow crops on it. I rent another hundred acres of tillable land because I need two hundred acres to grow enough feed for all the animals.

I get up at five in the morning and milk all the

It takes Craig two hours to milk the cows on his farm.

cows. Jersey milk is higher in protein and butterfat than milk from Holsteins, the type of cows most people milk. This makes Jersey milk especially good for cheese. All of my milk right now goes to making cheese.

It takes me about two hours to milk all the cows by machine. Then I come home and have breakfast before I clean up the milking parlor. After that, I clean up the barn and feed the cows, which takes another two hours. Then I do odd jobs. I might treat a sick cow, fix some machinery, plan strategy for the coming year, or do some computer work. I have all the cows on a computer so that I can keep track of the life history and breeding of each. The same goes for the corn and alfalfa fields. I keep track of the fertilizer that's been put on the fields, the chemicals, the yields, and the cutting and planting

11

Craig and his son hand-feed one of the newborn calves.

dates. At 3:30 P.M., I milk the cows again.

But I do more with the cows than just milk them. I also breed and sell them worldwide. My brother and sister own farms too, and between the three of us we've sold cows to Japan, Brazil, and India. Probably a quarter of my income comes from breeding.

Dairy cows should calve once a year. You breed them, and they have calves nine months later. A dairy cow bears milk 305 days a year and is dry for 60. This is the cow's "vacation," during which her body gets a rest. Afterward, she should be ready to mate again.

HOW I GOT STARTED:
I've been in this business all my life. I grew up on a farm in New Lebanon, New York, which is south of here. We milked four hundred cows a day there, and I was in a partnership with my father. Then, my wife and I decided to try it on our own, and we moved here. We built everything from scratch and went deep into debt. Now we're attempting to pay it all off.

HOW I FEEL ABOUT IT:
You shouldn't do this kind of work if you don't love it. I'm doing something different all the time. The only constant is that I'm always milking cows twice a day. But that's

okay with me because my cows are like my best friends.

Another thing I like is that I get to spend time with my kids, sometimes with them working right alongside me. That's a great feeling. And I love living in the country. It's a great place to bring up kids, and you get lots of fresh air here.

WHAT YOU SHOULD KNOW: Don't think that this job is drudgery. Sure, it's seven days a week, but you can hire some part-time help and get a day off here and there. And after one day off, I'm ready to get back to work.

It's a hard business for a young kid to get into, even one who knows something about it, because it requires such a big investment. The best thing to do is find an old farmer who doesn't have kids and try to get into a partnership with him.

You can do this right out of high school, but I suggest going to college. That way, you'll see whether there's something else you'd rather do. Also, you've got to be a businessman to be a farmer. You have to learn which grains and fertilizers will save you money. Enrolling in an agriculture program will help.

There's money to be made, but it sure isn't easy. We made a good living last year, spent a quarter of a million dollars on a new barn, and then this year the price of milk dropped, so we're hurting.

Kids I hire locally I start at minimum wage. One kid who has worked for me for five years gets $5.50 an hour.

Craig begins milking the cows at five in the morning.

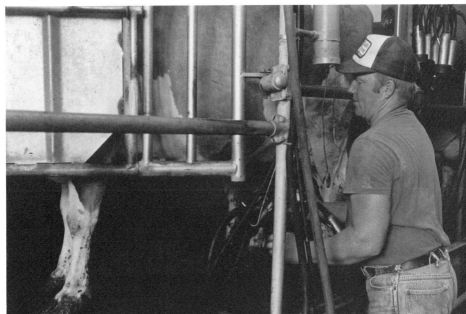

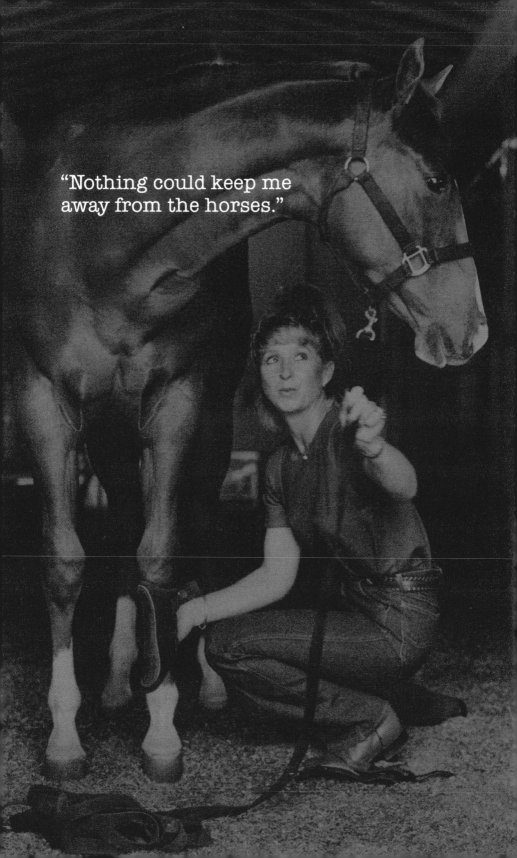

"Nothing could keep me away from the horses."

KELLEY K. MILLIGAN

HORSE SHOW MANAGER

Lake View Terrace, California

WHAT I DO:
I'm vice president of an equestrian center, which is a large facility where horses are boarded. People pay a monthly fee to use our arenas, trails, and stables. There are several advantages to keeping your horse at an equestrian center instead of in your backyard. For one, we feed and care for the horses. Also, the horse owners get to meet other owners and trainers. And we sponsor special events, too.

My specific responsibility is the organization of these special events, such as barbecues and hayrides, and the horse shows. A horse show is a competition that involves many different categories relating to the ability of the horse and the ability of the rider. I also manage the horses that we offer for sale.

Kelley spends as much time as possible with the horses.

We have special events two or three times a month, and there's an enormous amount of work that goes into each one. I have to arrange for the caterers, the photographers, the music, and the sound system. I also order the ribbons and the awards, hire the judge and the announcer, and arrange for the water truck, which is used to water down the track so dust doesn't ruin the show.

Show secretaries help me out by processing the entries for the competition. We often get kids to be show secretaries because it's a great way for them to learn organization and management.

HOW I GOT STARTED:
My father was a professional jockey, and then he became a professional trainer. Also, both my mother and grandmother competed in horse shows when they were little, so horses were in my family.

15

It seemed natural that I'd get involved with them. But when I was a child, I was allergic to horses! Until the age of 10, I couldn't be around them at all. Then my allergy let up, and I started to ride. After I got some experience, I was able to show horses in competition, which I did for about ten years as a hobby. Eventually I turned showing horses into a business, be- cause when a horse I showed won, people would want to buy it. So I started selling.

My father builds equestrian centers now. He's built four of the top facilities in California. After a while, I quit showing and began managing this center. You have to have a background in horses to become a manager, and I had the right background.

Kelley rides one of the horses that she boards at the center.

HOW I FEEL ABOUT IT:

I'm happier than I've ever been. I love showing, I love traveling to the world championships, and I love servicing the people here — that, to me, is the ultimate. We're offering something that makes people happy, and making people happy is better than winning any blue ribbon.

The main difficulty I have is my allergy. Even though I've gotten better, I'm still allergic to horses, and I have to take medication. But nothing could keep me away from horses.

WHAT YOU SHOULD KNOW:

I deal with a lot of people at the center who have never ridden before or who might have ridden before but have had bad experiences. I teach them the basics before they ever get on a horse. I try to make them feel safe. If you want to get involved with horses, you need to learn

Kelley plans all the special events at the center, including the barbecues, hayrides, and horse shows.

these things as a first step. So find a place that has a good reputation for teaching beginners.

If you think you want to have a career with horses, you have to find a stable or a farm where you can work or a trainer who will work with you. We plan to start a career program here, but the fact is, there is no set way to learn this business. Often, you have to work without pay in order to get experience. You have to apprentice in this business, and the earlier you start, the better. Then, once

you have the experience, you can get a job as an assistant at a stable, grooming horses, cleaning stalls, and exercising the horses.

In the beginning, the pay is minimal. But if you get good, you can go from $5 an hour as a stable hand to $10 an hour. As a first job, it's comparable to working in a department store, but you'll have a lot more fun. Training, you might make about $30,000 a year. At the top level, you can make $100,000. But that's the ultimate.

"Not everybody gets to work with a killer whale."

MANNY GARCIA

MARINE MAMMAL TRAINER

Miami, Florida

WHAT I DO:

I care for and train marine mammals at the Miami Seaquarium. I'm responsible for a killer whale named Lolita and a Pacific white-sided dolphin named Makani. A typical day for me includes playing with the animals, caring for their health, training them, and doing a show for visitors to the Seaquarium.

To train marine mammals, we use a method called positive reinforcement. If we ask an animal to do something and the animal does the task correctly, we give it a reward. The reward might be food, attention, or both. It all depends on the animal. Every animal is different.

It's not as difficult as most people think to train a dolphin to do a flip. Mostly it involves common sense and patience — a lot of patience. It's like working with kids in kindergarten. Dolphins have a short attention span, and they get bored, so you have to keep them motivated with new challenges. You have to work to make it fun for them. Some tricks never end up in a show. We develop them just to keep the animals mentally stimulated.

The time it takes to train an animal depends on the individual animal and the task you want to teach. Some tasks take a day or two, but a trick that requires the trainer and animal to work together can take much longer. In one trick, the trainer rides on the nose of the whale while it leaps straight up into the air. A trick like that can take a year to learn and another year to perfect. It's like riding a bike. You can learn in a few tries, but it takes you another year to get really good.

Manny performs a show each day with the killer whale Lolita.

A lot of the things we train are similar to natural behaviors that the animals already exhibit in the wild. For example, a flip comes naturally to a dolphin. But you can't expect a killer whale to do a flip. We don't make animals do anything that's unnatural for them.

The training is not just in flips and spirals, however. A lot of it involves teaching the animals to do things that help us to care for them. For example, when we show the whale a syringe, she dives down and gives us her tail so we can draw her blood. In the old days, we had to drain the tank and beach the whale when we needed a blood sample. It was a dangerous operation. Now it takes two minutes. So that's the first thing we train the whales to do now.

In addition to my work here, I also go out on rescues. Recently, there were six pilot whales beached in the Florida Keys. We went out, rescued them, and flew them here in a helicopter. That sort of thing is a neat experience. I've also been involved with manatee rescues. Manatees are an endangered species in Florida. There are only about 1,200 manatees left, so saving their lives is really important.

HOW I GOT STARTED:
I grew up in Miami and visited the Seaquarium as a child. I was fascinated by the idea of working there. As soon as I was old enough,

Manny develops relationships with the animals he trains.

Much of Manny's work involves caring for Lolita.

I took a job as a messenger just to get in. Six months later, there was an opening in the diving department, and they let me in. After two years, I began working with the dolphins. After another year, I was transferred to the killer whale. Now, I work part time with the killer whale and part time with the dolphins.

All the training I've had has been on the job. There is no school that teaches you marine mammal training. You have to learn by doing it.

HOW I FEEL ABOUT IT:
I love this work. Not everybody gets to work with a killer whale. I'd go crazy if I were locked up in an office. But it's not as glamorous as people might think. We do only two fifteen-minute shows a day, which means that the rest of the time you're doing a lot of scrubbing. And the whole time you're dealing with the cold, slimy fish we feed to the killer whales and dolphins.

WHAT YOU SHOULD KNOW:
To work at a place like this, you should be the kind of person who's good with kids. Because you do shows, you have to be personable, and you have to want to educate people. You also need a lot of patience to deal with the animals.

You can expect to make about $250 to $300 a week as a starting trainer. Later, if you stay with the business, you'll probably make between $30,000 and $35,000 a year.

"Banning wildlife imports impacts species in the farthest corners of the world."

GINETTE HEMLEY

WILDLIFE CONSERVATIONIST

Washington, D.C.

WHAT I DO:
I'm the director of TRAFFIC, which stands for Trade Records Analysis of Flora and Fauna in Commerce. We're an arm of the World Wildlife Fund. We assist in the enforcement of laws related to endangered species, which makes us a watchdog group. My job is to oversee the movement of wildlife products around the world, but we also monitor the levels of poaching and hunting.

A couple of years ago, we achieved a worldwide ban on the ivory trade. Now we're assessing its effect. Indications are that the poaching of African elephants is way down, but we're sending people out to assess the situation on a country-by-country basis.

Ginette displays a snakeskin that her organization has confiscated from poachers.

Here, in Washington, I work closely with government agencies, such as the Fish and Wildlife Service, to strengthen enforcement of the conservation laws. I also work with Congress to get new laws passed. Right now, for instance, I'm working on a piece of federal legislation designed to phase out the importation of wild birds, such as parrots. At the same time, though, we want to promote the captive breeding of these birds. On that side of the issue, we work closely with the pet industry.

One of the methods we use to monitor shipments of wildlife involves using Fish and Wildlife Service statistics to see what's coming into the country — skins, ivory, birds, fur, tropical fish — and where it's going. Then we check the legality of each shipment. For example, if we find out that a shipment of snake-skins is coming into New

York from Nigeria, which has a ban on such exports, we pass that information along to the Fish and Wildlife enforcement staff or to the Customs Department.

We often get tips from people who hear about these shipments. It might be people in the industry who are ratting on their competitors. Or it might be conservationists who have heard about some illegal activity. We also have a network of offices around the world that feed us information.

In addition to our own work, we fund and sponsor other projects in the field. We might give a grant to a biologist to study a pop-ulation of alligators or elephants and then use that study to support protective legislation. We're also involved in public awareness. We produce educational materials for schools and put out brochures for people traveling abroad.

HOW I GOT STARTED:
I have always been interested in science, even as a child. My father was a geologist, and he took me into the field with him. In college, I majored in biology and had a strong interest in ecology. After college, I came to Washington, D.C., and got a job as an intern at a conservation group. Through that, I met a lot of people in the

Ginette investigates some illegal wildlife products.

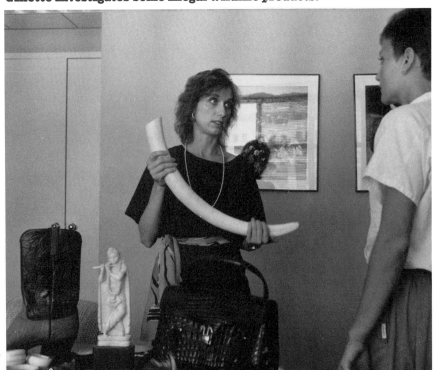

Ginette looks up some data on endangered species.

field, and eventually I ended up at TRAFFIC. I started out as a technician, doing computer coding for a data base on endangered species. Then I became a staff biologist, later an assistant director, and finally director.

HOW I FEEL ABOUT IT:
There's always something new cropping up, so I'm constantly stimulated. In fact, I'm often overwhelmed by the amount of work that needs to be done. Because I work outside the government, though, I'm allowed a lot of latitude. I'm not constrained by the bureaucracy. And the global focus of our agency has made me realize how interlinked all these issues really are. Banning imports of wildlife products into the United States impacts people and species in the farthest corners of the world.

WHAT YOU SHOULD KNOW:
Some background in the life sciences is important to understanding ecology and the interlinkings of people, wildlife, and plants. Learning languages other than English is also very important. In fact, half of our staff is fluent in a second language. Furthermore, you need an open mind to deal with different cultures and to understand the needs of the developing world. You really have to have a college degree in this field, but not necessarily an advanced degree – I don't have one.

The pay is getting increasingly competitive. Ten years ago, conservation was a career on the radical fringe. Now it's becoming more mainstream. Entry-level positions here, straight out of college, pay $25,000 to $30,000. But not all environmental groups pay this well.

"I'm teaching kids that what's good for animals is good for people too."

OKEEFENOKEE JOE
SNAKE HANDLER
Odum, Georgia

WHAT I DO:
I give lectures about snakes in schools. I also appear in television documentaries, including a series called "Know Your Snakes" and a show called "Swamp Wise." And I'm working on a network series about American wildlife called "Wild and Free."

I teach kids all about snakes: what they do, how they live, and how to identify the dangerous ones. But I don't teach children how to capture snakes or train them. Most people are afraid of snakes. Usually it's because they don't know anything about them. That's why I teach kids about snakes, so they will understand not to harm them.

I'm known as Okeefenokee Joe because I used to work at the Okeefenokee Swamp Park, taking care of the animals.

Okeefenokee Joe often lectures at schools and public libraries.

I was the only human inhabitant of the park. My neighbors were American black bear, deer, and gators, so the people in the area gave me that name. Now, Okeefenokee Joe is a kind of character that I take on when I do my act.

I've been doing the school talks for about fifteen years now throughout Georgia, South Carolina, and Florida. I give a forty-minute presentation that's a combination of entertainment and education. I call or write the schools to set up dates for my talks, then I make the appearances. Between February and May, I talk at about ninety-five schools, averaging three to four a day. About the only help I have is my wife, who types the contracts.

HOW I GOT STARTED:
From the time I was a kid, I've been interested in animals. I had raccoons,

opossums, snakes, and bobcats. I would capture them and domesticate them. My friends were mostly people who knew animals, so when I needed some information, I'd just ask someone how to care for a critter.

I didn't go right into the animal business, though. I made a living for years as a songwriter and performer. I played country music and had about eighty songs recorded. I traveled around the country and the world. And everywhere I went, I checked out zoos and roadside animal exhibits. I was always interested in animals, and I tried to keep learning about them.

Then I got a job at the Okeefenokee Swamp Park because I knew the fellow who ran the place. I started out as assistant to the assistant maintenance manager. Soon, however, they found out I knew a lot about animals, and I got promoted. Eventually I became curator.

As curator, I met thousands of people who visited the park each year, and it became obvious to me that these people had confused ideas about snakes. That's how I got the idea to start a teaching program to educate kids about snakes and how they are a necessary part of the animal kingdom.

Okeefenokee Joe handles many different kinds of snakes.

Okeefenokee Joe teaches children how snakes live.

HOW I FEEL ABOUT IT:

I like to think that kids really learn from my presentations. I think I'm helping to change their attitudes toward wildlife. Most people nowadays live in cities and know very little about wild animals. But as our domain grows, the animals' domain is diminishing, which is why we need to work like the dickens to preserve it. I'm helping kids realize that there is still some wilderness out there and that we have to preserve it. If all the rain forests disappear and we continue to pollute our environment, the earth will die. So what's good for the animals is good for people, too. That's what I'm teaching.

WHAT YOU SHOULD KNOW:

If you want to do this kind of work, be prepared to be poor. It's hard to make a living working with animals. I know people with degrees in zoology who can't get a job.

If you love animals, though, you should pursue a career with them. I think experience is the best teacher. Get it however you can. Volunteer at a zoo. There may not be much money in this field, but there is a great need for people to work in it. All the states now are interested in preserving what little wildlife they have left, and they need help. For most of these jobs, you need a college degree. But I don't have that degree, and I've done it.

"As a child I was always trying to bring new animals home."

LAUREL WRIGHT

VETERINARIAN

Tacoma, Washington

WHAT I DO:
I'm a veterinarian in private practice, which means that I go to my office each day and treat animals that people bring to me. Another doctor shares the practice with me, and we have about ten employees. They include receptionists, kennel help, and animal technicians, who are essentially nurses.

I spent most of the day seeing appointments. Sometimes, puppies and kittens are brought in for vaccinations; other times, I see sick or injured animals. We handle everything from routine treatments to emergencies. I also spend part of the day in surgery — doing spayings, neuterings, removing bladder stones, and fixing broken legs.

Veterinarians are broadly grouped into large animal vets and small animal vets.

Laurel gives one of her patients a routine check-up.

I'm a small animal vet. I deal mostly with dogs, cats, rodents, birds, and reptiles. A large animal vet is someone who goes out on farm calls and treats cows, horses, and pigs.

HOW I GOT STARTED:
I had pets as a child, and I was always trying to convince my parents to let me bring new animals home. I also knew early on that I liked the idea of becoming a doctor. In high school, I volunteered at a local veterinary hospital. I also took lots of science courses. Then I applied to a special veterinary program, which combined college and graduate school, so it took me only seven years to finish instead of the usual eight. But my case is an exception. Typically, you need a four-year bachelor's degree before you begin a four-year graduate veterinary program.

31

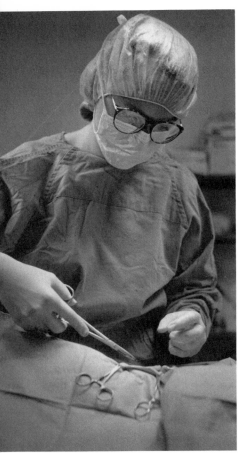

Laurel performs surgery on one of the animals in her care.

On the downside, you see a certain amount of neglect and ignorance, and that's hard to deal with. Sometimes, people try to treat their own animals and end up making matters worse. Other times, you treat an animal that has been accidentally shot, or one that never got its vaccinations and is now suffering from a disease.

WHAT YOU SHOULD KNOW: It's important to love animals, of course. But you also need to be fascinated by medicine. Having pets is certainly a good first experience, but it's even better to volunteer at a clinic. A lot of vets will let you tag along and watch them work. At a clinic, you might help clean cages or do some other dirty work, but you'll also get to watch everything from exams to surgery.

I would recommend getting as much experience with animals as you can. There's a program in this area, for example, through which kids can volunteer at the humane society.

In college, you should structure your program around the sciences. Take lots of biology and chemistry. And work hard, because those grades are weighed especially heavily when you apply to veterinary school. You might even major in zoology or animal science.

HOW I FEEL ABOUT IT: On the positive side, I feel really challenged by the medical aspect of my job, and I like the hands-on work — I like doing surgery. I also like helping people with their pets. Some people think that vets work only with animals and not with people. But that isn't true. People become attached to their pets, so you have to spend a lot of time dealing with the pet owners and their feelings.

The money in this business depends on where you're located as well as on the kind of work you go into. If you own your own practice, you could probably make about $60,000 to $80,000 a year. As an employee vet — someone who works for another vet's practice — you'll make about $40,000.

But you don't have to work in a practice. There are other aspects of veterinary medicine you might want to go into. Some vets, for example, are employed by drug companies that do research involving animals. These vets monitor the health of the animals involved in laboratory tests. Others go into regulatory medicine, which involves working for the government. You might be monitoring a food inspection program, controlling exotic diseases, or doing research. Some of these positions pay quite well.

Laurel examines some slides in her laboratory.

"From the time I was a child, I was always a real animal lover."

TUFAIL MOHAMMED

ANIMAL SHELTER FOREMAN

New York, New York

WHAT I DO:
I oversee a staff of ten kennel people in the shelter operations department of an animal shelter in New York City. My responsibilities involve caring for the animals while they are here. The shelter also has education, adoption, animal rescue, medical, and legal departments. The administration deals with finance and public relations.

In the morning, I assign tasks to my staff, and at the end of the day I make sure the work has been done. Kennel people are responsible for keeping the animal cages clean, assisting the public in adopting animals, and taking in animals that people bring to us. They also feed the animals and help the doctor administer treatment when necessary.

Tufail cares for animals at the shelter until they are adopted.

I'm a working supervisor, so I'll often assign myself to clean one of the wards first thing in the morning. Once that's done, I may answer bells, which is our term for assisting the public. Feeding time is 2:00 P.M., and that's when the kennel people assigned to feeding duty leave what they're doing to feed the animals. The day ends at 4:00 P.M.

We deal primarily with dogs and cats here, but we also get some more unusual animals, such as birds, snakes, and rodents. We even get farm animals occasionally, such as sheep and ducks. How does a city shelter end up with farm animals? Well, it's illegal to keep a farm animal in an apartment, but some people try it anyway. If a neighbor complains, however, or the authorities find out some other way, animal rescue drivers collect the animal and bring it here.

Tufail takes a dog from his cage so it can be cleaned.

The minute we get an unusual animal, we call a licensed rehabilitator to remove it. It's the rehabilitator's job to arrange for the animal to be sent to a place where it can be legally kept, such as a farm. For dogs and cats, we have our own adoption service.

HOW I GOT STARTED:
I came to the United States from Trinidad, and this was my first job here. In Trinidad, I was always around animals from the time I was a child, and I was a real animal lover. So, when I saw this job advertised, I thought it would be a good thing for me to do. Ani-

mals were my hobby at home, but they're my career here.

HOW I FEEL ABOUT IT:
This is interesting work if you love animals, because you get to meet a lot of people who share your interest, and you can exchange views with them as to how particular animals should be treated. Sometimes you can have quite lively exchanges.

We have a policy relating to dangerous animals, however, that I don't care for. It's that we have to work with every animal to make it fit for another adoption. Now, I'm not afraid of dealing with aggressive animals — I always show respect for animals, whether they're docile or not — but sometimes you get animals that are dangerously aggressive, and you can tell they will continue to be so. In these cases, I believe it's appropriate to put the animal to sleep. This is the hardest part of the work.

WHAT YOU SHOULD KNOW: If you're thinking about working in this field, you should be someone who has a lot of patience. If you're dealing with an animal, you have to win its confidence, and that takes time. Also, you should learn as much as you can about the particular animals you want to work with. At the shelter, for instance, we have a multitude of cats and dogs. If you want to work here, you should read literature about cats and dogs, and learn as much as you can about them. You don't need formal training to become a kennel worker. But if you want to become a professional, training is essential.

The salary plan at this shelter is very diversified. It depends on what job you have. Some jobs pay very well; others are not so well paid. Some people do this just as a job. Others are here because they love animals.

Tufail assists a doctor as he examines a sick cat.

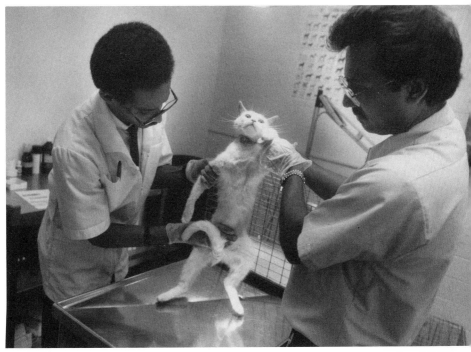

"I buy every book I can find on animals."

ANDREA TACHIERA

ILLUSTRATOR

El Cerrito, California

WHAT I DO:
I create illustrations of animals for advertising agencies, book publishers, greeting card publishers, and various other clients. I have slowly come to specialize in animal illustrations. I've done a poster for an insect zoo in San Francisco and T-shirt designs for Yosemite National Park. I've also done a series of animal coloring books that are sold in bookstores, aquariums, and zoos.

Drawing animals involves a lot of preparation. For instance, when I did the insect poster for the zoo, the curator let me take home trays of preserved bugs so I could study them. For other projects, I do research in libraries, and I buy every book I can find on animals. I search for images of the animals, but also for informa-

Andrea works on an illustration for a children's book on animals.

tion about the habitats I have to draw so that my illustrations can be accurate.

I'm a freelancer, so my workday is pretty unstructured, and that's how I like it. One day, I might spend the afternoon running errands or shopping for groceries and then work that night until two in the morning. Because I'm a freelancer, I set my own hours. So if it's a beautiful day, I have the opportunity to go out and enjoy it, then work at night or on the weekend to make up the time.

The work usually begins with an assignment from an art director. Generally, the art director gives you some parameters for the illustrations: size, style, subject matter, and so on. Then you do some sketches, which have to be approved. Sometimes you have to do a color sketch. Then you do the finished painting. You're always work-

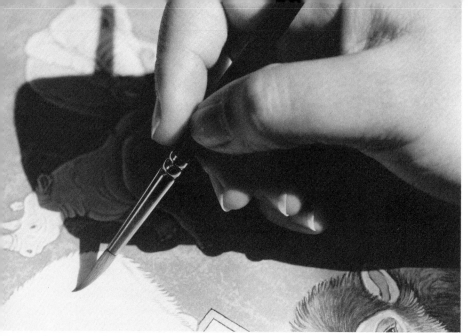

Andrea paints a watercolor for an advertisement.

ing under a deadline, but some jobs have much shorter deadlines than others. For example, advertising jobs require a quick turnaround, while books usually have a more drawn-out schedule.

HOW I GOT STARTED:
I always drew as a child, especially animals, because I never cared much for drawing people. In college, however, I got a degree in architecture because I was told you couldn't make a living as an artist.

But I was never very good at architecture. Next, I tried working as a graphic artist, but I felt that lacked creativity. So I started taking night classes in illustration and eventually attended art school full time.

My degree in illustration is a commercial art degree because illustration is not a fine art. Instead, it's a specific skill. The emphasis is on composition, color, drawing ability, and imagination. I started freelancing right away because it's hard to find a full-time job as an illustrator. I've been doing it for five years now.

HOW I FEEL ABOUT IT:
I like the freedom of being a freelancer. You get to work with a lot of different people, so if you don't get along with one client, you don't have to work with that person again. It's not like having a boss whom you have to see every day. I also like working at home. But sometimes the hours are horrendous —

eighty or ninety a week. And you can't leave your work behind at the office because you live there.

WHAT YOU SHOULD KNOW: Many successful illustrators don't have art-related degrees, but you really have to know the field thoroughly to succeed without one. Personally, I would recommend going to school and getting an illustration degree. This is a competitive field, and more illustrators graduate from the art schools every year. You need a solid education behind you to compete. It's best to have a four-year bachelor's degree in illustration or commercial art from an accredited art college.

As far as freelancing goes, if you're not comfortable working by yourself, you might not like it. It requires a lot of self-discipline to dig in and do the work when it needs to be done. I know some people from school who were great artists and good students, but they couldn't handle the self-discipline.

The money fluctuates wildly. Advertising work pays the most, but it's also the most stressful and the least creative. Agencies will pay you a fortune for two days' work, but you won't sleep for those two days, and you probably won't eat. Publishing is probably the lowest paying work, but the deadlines are more flexible, and there's more creativity. In advertising, the pay can range from $500 to $10,000 for a ten-day project, depending on the client. In publishing, you might get $3,000 for a children's book that takes you months.

Andrea looks through some of her finished works.

"I hand-pick all the animals for my store."

JOSEPH CHORNOCK
PET SHOP OWNER
Germantown, Maryland

WHAT I DO:
I'm the sole proprietor of a full-service pet store. I have seven employees. Usually I come in to the store around ten in the morning. Some days I'll be here until nine at night, but other days I'll leave as early as three in the afternoon. Still, the store is a seven-day-a-week worry, even though I don't come in every day.

My first tasks in the morning are to take care of the previous day's receipts and to get my orders together for the different suppliers I deal with. Then I might go out to pick up a supply of pets. Distributors of pets will deliver, but I prefer to go to them myself so I can hand-pick the animals for my store.

I don't have dogs in the store because of space limitations. You can put four or

Joe answers a customer's questions about a new pet.

five kittens in one cage, but you can't do that with German shepherd puppies. If customers ask for dogs, though, I can order them.

We have a special kitten service here. When people's cats have kittens they can't keep, they bring them here, and we try to find homes for them. We make sure they're healthy and that they get good homes. We probably gave away over a thousand kittens last year. It's a community service, but it's also good business, because new pet owners will often come back to us for their supplies.

HOW I GOT STARTED:
The first job I ever had was helping a friend open a pet store. That was when I was 15. After that, I worked at a couple of other pet stores until I graduated from high school. Then, I traveled around the world for a year, and when I came back, I got

Joe makes sure that the birds are well cared for.

a job working for a grocery chain while I went to college and got a two-year business-administration degree.

For fifteen years, I worked at the grocery chain, and I learned ordering and merchandising there. Then, I decided to do something on my own, and I chose this business because I knew it the best. It took me about nine months of pounding the street to put together the capital for a store, but I finally convinced the banks that I knew what I was doing.

HOW I FEEL ABOUT IT:
I love my job, but there are some difficulties you have when you're working with animals. If you're selling shoes, shoes aren't going to die on you. But animals can, so I have to make sure that all the livestock is well cared for. All my employees have to know that if they don't feed and water the parakeets, they'll have twenty-five dead birds on their hands.

This type of thing has happened to me before. A tank of fish died, for example, because somebody didn't do his job. These creatures rely on us to keep them alive and healthy. If we do that, they'll bring us profits in return. If we don't, then we'll go out of business.

Sometimes I have problems with employees taking off work without notice. If three people are out on vacation, and we're running the store with a skeleton crew, I have to put my personal desires aside because I have the ultimate responsibility for my store. On the other hand, if I want to walk out of here at two in the afternoon, I can. There's nobody to tell me what I can or cannot do. In fact, I don't know if I could ever work for someone else again on a daily basis because I really like the freedom.

WHAT YOU SHOULD KNOW:
If you think you want to own a pet store, you should take the time to learn the business. Work for somebody else. There's so much to learn. We have a training program here for new employees, and during the first four weeks, we just teach them. They have to learn how to handle snakes, kittens – all the animals. I also sell pets to employees at cost so they can learn how to care for them at home.

As the owner of a small pet store you might make $25,000 a year for the first few years. Then, after you're established, that may go up to $30,000, or it may be $250,000, depending on the size of the store, the volume of business you do, the location, and so on.

Joe helps a young customer decide on a new pet.

"There's great satisfaction in making a dirty, matted dog look elegant."

MAREA TULLY

PET GROOMER

Duxbury, Massachusetts

WHAT I DO:

I bathe, brush, comb, and clip pets. I groom dogs and cats almost exclusively, but once I did a guinea pig. I work out of a shop in my home. Most people come to me by word of mouth, but I also run an ad in the Yellow Pages. I have three employees, and we do fifteen to seventeen dogs a day, plus a few cats. But this number can vary because some animals require a lot more time than others, depending on the breed.

For example, a Labrador has a short coat, so the grooming goes quickly. But an old English sheepdog might take three hours. Also, different people want different services. Some only want their dogs bathed. Others want the whole nine yards: bathing, flea shampoo, nails cut, ears cleaned, and the

Marea puts the finishing touches on a show poodle.

clipping. We'll also do a flea dip if a customer asks. This is stronger than a shampoo, but we don't like to do it because it's very toxic.

We've been in this location for thirteen years now, and I have a steady clientele. Some of my clients are on their second dog with me. I start work at 8:00 A.M. and try to finish by 5:00 P.M. But I have to be flexible because I have to work around my clients' schedules. I live thirty miles outside of Boston, and people who work in the city will drop off their dogs at 7:30 A.M. and pick them up again late in the afternoon.

When a customer brings me a really fine animal, I ask if I can use the dog for competitions. It has to be the best of its breed and well behaved. I groom the dog for free several times in exchange for its use during a show.

Twice a year I go to the New England Dog Groomers

Marea feeds one of the dogs after his grooming.

Association show, and I usually go to New York for Intergroom, an international competition and seminar. These events are strictly for grooming, as opposed to dog shows where they look for breeding.

HOW I GOT STARTED:
I grew up in England, where my family always had dogs, mostly mixed breeds. But we had a neighbor who owned show dogs. She raised corgis, and I got interested in show dogs through her. Later, when I was working in Ohio as a secretary, I took a grooming class and started grooming my own dogs for show. Eventually I put an ad in the paper to groom other dogs, and people started calling. That was twenty-two years ago, and I've been doing it ever since.

HOW I FEEL ABOUT IT:
There's great satisfaction to be had in taking a dirty, matted dog and making it elegant. It makes you feel good when the customer comes in and says, "Oh, he's beautiful!" It's a real ego boost.

And, of course, I enjoy the animals themselves. They get to know me. And when they come back to the shop, some of them remember which cage they were in and want to be put there again.

On the downside, it gets noisy having seventeen dogs in one room all day long. If one starts barking, they all start barking. Also, this is demanding physical work. Many dogs don't enjoy being done, so you have to hold them down with one arm while you groom them with the other. Groomers tend to suffer from carpal tunnel syndrome, which is caused by the repetitive motion of brushing. It affects the nerves in the forearms and fingers. Your muscles begin to cramp, and you can lose the feeling in your hands. Typically, this hits you after twenty years or so.

WHAT YOU SHOULD KNOW: There are schools now that teach the basics of grooming, including management and shop set-up. Most have three-month and six-month courses. After that, I would recommend doing an apprenticeship. Some people think that once they get out of school, they're dog groomers. But you can't learn all 128 breeds of dogs in three months. It takes a lot more time before you're able to open up your own shop.

This is not what you would normally consider very high-paying work. For a complete treatment, we charge $35. The groomer gets only half of that for about an hour and a half of work. In the South, the pay is even lower. New England and California are probably the best-paying areas for dog grooming.

Marea washes, clips, and brushes all the dogs.

"I keep track of all the gorillas in North America."

DAN WHARTON

ZOO BIOLOGIST

New York, New York

WHAT I DO:
I work for a zoo, gathering information about the animals so that the keepers can make informed decisions about their care. My department, Animal Management Services, maintains a library as well as an archive in which we keep records of all the animals. We also oversee keeper training and handle shipping arrangements for the animals.

In addition to my work for the zoo, I'm also a member of the Gorilla Species Survival Plan Committee, a group set up by the American Association of Zoological Parks and Aquariums to manage the gorilla population in America's zoos. My title is Gorilla Stud Book Keeper. It's my job to keep track of all the gorillas in North America. In my data

Dan looks up some information on a species of giant panda.

base, I log in each animal's birthday, place of origin, reproductive status, behavioral traits, and social group. Then, twice a year, the committee meets to fine tune our master plan for the preservation of the species.

It's entirely possible that, in the future, the only gorillas left will be the ones we're breeding in captivity. In this way, we're an insurance policy against the extinction of the species as a whole.

People used to think that it was enough just to know that a species such as the Siberian tiger was endangered — that all you had to do was breed as many Siberian tigers as you could in captivity. But now zoos around the country realize that endangered species will be protected only through joint efforts and planning. Once a population starts to die out, somebody has to give direction as to how many animals to breed and when. That's why zoos are now working together to manage their animal populations.

HOW I GOT STARTED:
I grew up in a rural area, and my family had everything from cows to sheep. We were also beekeepers. Because I was around so many animals, it wasn't long before I became interested in animal breeding and also in wildlife. I was very young when I knew that I wanted to go into this field.

In college, I got my degree in psychology, with an emphasis in biology. Then, in graduate school, I got a master's in international administration focusing on environmental organizations and a Ph.D. in biology. After that, I was in the Peace Corps for a while, and then I won a Fulbright Scholarship to study zoo biology issues in Germany. I also did an internship in Africa and picked up a couple of foreign languages along the way.

HOW I FEEL ABOUT IT:
This is probably the most exciting work that a person with my interests can do. I believe that zoos really make a difference in wildlife conservation, because a lot of the work that zoos do today will determine which species

Dan reviews one of the files on animals in his care.

Dan manages the gorilla population in America's zoos.

will survive for future centuries. The Przewalski horse, for instance, is extinct in the wild but still exists in captivity in healthy numbers. And the Pere David deer is another famous example.

If there is a downside, it's seeing clearly what needs to be done and not being able to do all of it. To most of us who do this kind of work, it's clear that much more needs to be done, but the manpower and funding are limited.

WHAT YOU SHOULD KNOW: This is a very competitive field, but even so, there's always room for good people. You can pursue any number of formal educational routes to get here. The study of

animal science is a very good one for a prospective zoo biologist. But informal study is also very important. It's good, for instance, to become involved with animals in some way. Do farm work, or take a special interest in pet care. If you have a parakeet, for example, learn everything there is to know about it: where parakeets come from, how they are bred in captivity, what their nutritional requirements are, and so on.

Nobody gets rich working for a zoo, but people do make a decent living. There are some zoo directors who make over $100,000 a year. Most curators, however, are probably in the $20,000 to $50,000 a year range.

"We're responsible for all the wildlife in the state."

MILES YOUNG

GAME WARDEN

Martinez, California

WHAT I DO:

I'm a patrol lieutenant for the California Department of Fish and Game, which is responsible for all the wildlife in the state. Patrol lieutenants are the police officers of the department. We regulate the taking of sport game and police the illegal animal trade.

Most people think game wardens just ride around the countryside checking deer licenses, but we do a lot more than that. The department is involved in preserving natural habitats, for example. So when someone wants to put a bridge across a stream, we get involved. A biologist checks out the site, then the property owners are told how to build the bridge so that it will cause the least possible damage to the environment. We also deal with pollution.

Miles was a policeman before taking a job with Fish and Game.

If a tanker truck empties its gas into a creek, we're called in.

We also check airports and boats for illegal shipments of wildlife. The Customs Service checks cruise ships coming in from Mexico, but sometimes we check them, too. And we check markets and restaurants that deal in fish and shellfish to make sure the fish they have were legally obtained. We work hand in hand with the health department on this. If I find tons of fish that were legally obtained but are now rotting, I'll turn the matter over to the health department. If the health department finds healthy but illegally obtained fish, they'll call me.

And we do much more. We assist biologists when they do deer counts. We teach hunter education classes. And, as law enforcement officers, we also spend some time testifying in court.

Miles checks the waterfront for wildlife shipments.

Every warden in the state is involved in these things, but the emphasis is different in different places. In San Francisco, we just picked up a spitting cobra at the airport that came in from Pakistan. Someone was trying to bring it in as a pet. A warden on Mount Shasta, however, spends more time on deer and duck patrols.

HOW I GOT STARTED: Because I'm an outdoors person, I always wanted to work for Fish and Game. In

college, I pursued a major in police science as a way of getting a job with the department.

After I graduated from college, I went to Vietnam for a couple of years. Then, when I came back, I applied here, but there were very few openings, which is still the case. So I worked for the San Francisco Police Department for six years until some jobs at Fish and Game opened up. There were three thousand applicants for just ten jobs, but I got one of them.

HOW I FEEL ABOUT IT:

You have to love this work because you don't get rich doing it. If I had stayed with the police department, I'd be making a lot more money. But I got tired of police work, because it seemed as though the same people were always arresting the same other people. I felt that by working with animals I could do more for myself personally and also for the fish and wildlife.

Now I often feel like I'm in a war — a wildlife war — because this is still a law enforcement job, and you can get shot at or knifed. It's dangerous because sometimes there's a lot of money at stake. Poaching is extremely profitable. A handful of bear gall bladder, which is used in Chinese medicine, can be sold for the same amount as a handful of heroin. The penalty, however, is much less for killing a bear than for selling heroin.

WHAT YOU SHOULD KNOW:

A game warden's job is to protect and preserve the state's natural resources. That includes protecting the state's wildlife, but it doesn't mean you interfere with hunting. You have to accept that there is legal killing. You also have to be able to appreciate the needs and problems of commercial fishermen.

To do this work, you have to be in good physical shape. One night, you might be out on the water; the next, you might be in the hills chasing a poacher. You also have to have a dedication to duty because a game warden is always on call. All wardens have districts for which they're responsible, whether they're on vacation or not.

I can live on the pay, but I'll never get rich on it. An entry-level Fish and Game warden makes about $1,600 a month.

Miles looks through a catch for illegal shellfish.

"I hadn't really thought about basing a career on my knowledge of horses."

FELICITAS CAMACHO

MAGAZINE EDITOR

Hinsdale, Illinois

WHAT I DO:

I edit a monthly magazine for people interested in horses. I'm responsible for putting out every issue. Advertisements are a big part of what I do. I work with two other people on the advertising staff, and together we come up with a theme for each issue. Then, we target advertisers who have products or services related to that theme.

I start at 9:00 A.M. making ad calls, and that takes most of the morning. In the afternoon, I call writers to check up on their stories. Our deadline is the twentieth of each month, and it's my responsibility to make sure that everything is in by that date.

I'm usually at the office until about 4:00 P.M. But I'm not here every day. Some days

I might drive to another town to check out a lead on a story — a new stallion farm, say, or another horse-related business. After my visit, I'll decide whether or not to assign a story about it.

Another big part of my job is promoting the magazine. During stallion season, for example, which begins in November, we run a lot of stallion stories in the magazine. When I go out to visit stallion farms or go to shows, I make sure that the magazine is distributed at these places.

HOW I GOT STARTED:

I rode horses when I was in school, and I joined the equestrian club in college. Still, I hadn't really thought about basing a career on my knowledge of horses. After I got my degree in English, however, I heard about this job, which seemed to tie together my interests. The

Felicitas gets to work with all different kinds of horses.

Felicitas visits a stable to check out a lead on a story.

magazine wanted somebody who could write and at the same time knew about horses.

HOW I FEEL ABOUT IT:
I don't know whether I'll do this for the rest of my life, but I enjoy it now. I'm in the field a lot, going to horse shows and clinics, and I like that. I also get to ride all kinds of unusual horses, such as a Paso Fino, which is a small horse known for its smooth gait. You can ride a Paso Fino at full gallop and still hold a glass of champagne without spilling it. There are other satisfactions, too, such as the control over the design and the content of the magazine.

WHAT YOU SHOULD KNOW:
If you're interested in working with horses, join clubs and organizations, such as the 4H Club and the Pony Club. That will help you meet other people in the field and further your knowledge of horses and the horse industry. Also, some universities offer equestrian courses for college credit. Most of the ones I know about are in Missouri or Kentucky. You could also do an internship as a stable helper or groom at a horse farm.

Generally, I would advise people who have a love for animals to get some skills to back up that love. In my case, it was my skill with English that helped me land this job.

As far as working for a magazine goes, the salary is typically in the mid-twenties, depending on the size of the magazine. National magazines pay better.

Related Careers

Here are more animal-related careers you may want to explore:

ANIMAL BEHAVIORIST
Animal behaviorists train animals to obey the commands of their owners.

ANIMAL SHOW JUDGE
Animal show judges rate animals on their breeding, grooming, and behavior in competitions.

ANIMAL NUTRITIONIST
Animal nutritionists determine the dietary requirements of pets and then design pet foods to meet those requirements.

CIRCUS TRAINER
Circus trainers teach wild animals to perform tricks, including standing on two legs and jumping through hoops.

FISH FARMER
Fish farmers breed and raise different species of fish to sell as food.

JOCKEY
Jockeys are professional horse riders who compete in races for cash purses.

MARINE BIOLOGIST
Marine biologists study aquatic plants and animals.

PEDIGREE BREEDER
Pedigree breeders raise pure breeds of animals, such as dogs or horses, for sale to the public.

RIDING INSTRUCTOR
Riding instructors give lessons in how to ride and jump horses.

SAFARI GUIDE
Safari guides lead people on tours of jungle habitats, providing information about the animals and the terrain.

STABLE MANAGER
Stable managers are responsible for managing, feeding, grooming, and otherwise caring for horses being boarded at their stable.

WILDLIFE PHOTOGRAPHER
Wildlife photographers specialize in taking pictures of wildlife subjects.

Organizations

Contact these organizations for information about the following careers:

ANIMAL NUTRITIONIST
American Academy of Veterinary Nutrition
c/o IAMS, 2395 Clower Street, Snellville, GA 30278

MARINE MAMMAL TRAINER
American Association of Zoological Parks and Aquariums
Oglebay Park, Wheeling, WV 26003

DAIRY FARMER
American Dairy Association
6300 North River Road, Rosemont, IL 60018

FISH FARMER
American Fisheries Society
5410 Grosvenor Lane, Suite 110, Bethesda, MD 20814

HORSE SHOW MANAGER
American Horse Council
1700 K Street, N.W., Suite 300, Washington, DC 20006

ZOO KEEPER
American Ornithologist Union
National Museum of Natural History, Washington, DC 20560

ZOO BIOLOGIST
American Society of Zoologists
104 Sirius Circle, Thousand Oaks, CA 91360

VETERINARIAN
American Veterinary Medical Association
1931 North Meacham Road, Schaumburg, IL 60173

ANIMAL SHELTER FOREMAN
ASPCA Animal Rescue
2336 Linden Boulevard, Brooklyn, NY 11208

GAME WARDEN
International Association of Fish and Wildlife Agencies
444 North Capitol Street, N.W., #534, Washington, DC 20001

PET GROOMER
International Professional Groomers
79 Flint Locke Drive, Duxbury, MA 02332

ILLUSTRATOR
Society of Illustrators
128 East 63rd Street, New York, NY 10021

Books

ANIMAL DOCTORS: WHAT DO THEY DO?
By Carla Greene. New York: Harper & Row, 1967.

THE ART AND BUSINESS OF PROFESSIONAL GROOMING
By Dorothy Walin. Loveland, Co.: Alpine Publications, 1986.

BEHIND THE SCENES AT THE ZOO
By George Zappler. Garden City, N.Y.: Doubleday, 1977.

CAREERS AT A ZOO
By Mark Lerner. Minneapolis, Minn.: Lerner Publications, 1980.

CAREERS FOR DOG LOVERS
By Lynn Hall. Chicago: Follett Publishing, 1978.

CAREERS IN AGRICULTURE
By Christopher Benson. Minneapolis, Minn.: Lerner Publications, 1975.

CAREERS IN BIOLOGICAL SCIENCE
By Paul Sarnoff. New York: Julian Messner, 1968.

CAREERS IN CONSERVATION
By Ada Graham. San Francisco: Sierra Club Books, 1980.

CAREERS IN THE ANIMAL KINGDOM
By Walter G. Olesky. New York: Julian Messner, 1968.

CAREERS WORKING WITH ANIMALS
By Guy R. Hodge. Washington, D.C.: Acropolis Books, 1979.

A DAY IN THE LIFE OF A VETERINARIAN
By William Jaspersohn. Boston: Little, Brown, 1978.

HALT! I'M A FEDERAL GAME WARDEN
By Willie J. Parker. New York: David McKay, 1977.

KEEPERS AND CREATURES AT THE ZOO
By Peggy Thompson. New York: Crowell, 1988.

THE STANDARD BOOK OF DOG GROOMING
By Diane Fenger. Fairfax, Va.: Denlinger's, 1983.

Glossary Index

animal shelter foreman, 34

brooder room — a heated room used for raising young birds, 7

calve — to give birth to a calf, 12

conservation — the careful preservation and protection of the natural environment, 23-25, 52

dairy farmer, 10

domesticate — to tame an animal so that it is capable of interacting safely with people, 28

ecology — the branch of science concerned with the relationship between animals and their environments, 24-25

equestrian — relating to horseback riding, 15-16, 59-60

game warden, 54

heifer — a young cow, especially one that has not yet had a calf, 11

horse show manager, 14

illustrator, 38

incubate — to nurture an egg in conditions favorable to hatching, 7

magazine editor, 58

marine mammal trainer, 18

neuter — to sterilize a male animal, 31

ornithology — the branch of zoology related to birds, 9

pet groomer, 46

pet shop owner, 42

poaching — the illegal capture of fish or game, 23, 57

snake handler, 26

spay — to sterilize a female animal, 31

veterinarian, 30

wildlife conservationist, 22

zoo biologist, 50

zoo keeper, 6